GHOSTS

Also by the Author

GHOSTS

AND OTHER UNSEEN VISITORS

Medium Robin May

SRP

Star Rising Publishers
Sedona, Arizona

The author of this book does not dispense medical
advise or prescribe the use of any technique as a form
of treatment for physical or medical problems without
the advice of a physician, either directly or indirectly.
The intent of the author is only to offer information
of a general nature to help you in your quest for health
and well-being. In the even you use any of the information in this book for yourself, which is your consti-
tutional right, the author and the publisher assume no
responsibility for your actions.

**Library of Congress Cataloging-in-Publication
Data**
Medium Robin May,
ghosts, and other unseen visitors/ Medium Robin May

Tradepaper: ISBN-13: 978-1893774612
Hardcover: ISBN-13: 978-1893774636

1st edition, August 2011 - Printed in The USA

CONTENTS

Introduction

Real encounters with ghosts, demons and other unseen visitors make for the largest part of this book. So if you are not familiar with ghosts, demons and other unseen visitors I would suggest you start at the beginning.

If you are familiar with ghosts, demons and other unseen visitors and just want to know what you can do about it, skip to the back of this book where you will find everything you need.

I have written everything as simply as possible so that you could understand what I am saying. I have included a small definition section so you can become familiar with some of the words I have used. Also in the back you will find an index so you can look up words quickly.

The intent is to give you all the information you will need to keep your family safe and protected from ghosts, demons and other unseen visitors without having to rely on outside sources.

CHAPTER 1
Understanding

Ghosts

Demons

& the

Unseen

Understanding

There are unlimited dimensions within unlimited dimensions, the universe is setup this way. Take two mirrors and place one in front of you and then place one behind you, what do you see? You see an infinite mirror image of yourself within the mirrors. This is the how the universe is setup. It is the same in the seen and unseen worlds.

The unseen world where ghosts and other unseen visitors reside is made the same way. The world of the unseen runs right next to the world of the living. The only thing that separates the world of the living with the world of ghosts and other unseen visitors is physical matter. The reason for the merging of worlds sometimes is quite simple. When a ghost wants to make contact and the will (determination) is strong enough the encounter happens. Will and emotion are in both worlds. The world of ghosts is a lighter version of our physical world, of course without the physical element.

For an encounter to happen, will and determination come into play. This also applies to those not so nice encounters.

Often when there are strong emotions at the time of death an object, place or person may be imprinted with the energy of the recently de-ceased. The ghost can linger, by choice. The lon-ger the ghost stays in the physical realm, the hard-er it is for the ghost to move on.

Ghosts

When you leave the physical world through death there are three things that happen. First you die and leave your physical body. Second, you shed your astral body. Third, you go to the light through the tunnel. This happens within a three day period. Contact at this time is very strong.

A ghost will go through the first step and some-times even the second step and then decide to stay in the physical world. Why? It could be unfinished business or a strong emotional tie to the physical world. Free will is in both the physical and the unseen world.

So a ghost is a person that dies and chooses not to continue to the next world.

Definition of ghosts:

In traditional belief, a ghost is the soul or spirit of a deceased person or animal that can appear, in visible form or other manifestation, to the liv-ing. Descriptions of the apparition of ghosts vary widely: The mode of manifestation can range from an invisible presence to translucent or wispy shapes, to realistic, life-like visions. The deliberate attempt to contact the spirit of a deceased person is known as necromancy, or in spiritism as a séance.

The belief in manifestations of the spirits of the dead is widespread, dating back to animism or ancestor worship in pre-literate cultures. Certain religious practices—funeral rites, exorcisms, and some practices of spiritualism and ritual magic—are specifically designed to appease the spirits of the dead. Ghosts are generally described as solitary essences that haunt particular locations, objects, or people they were associated with in life, though stories of the phantom armies, ghost trains, phantom ships, and even ghost animals have also been recounted.

Demons

Demons are very different. Demons are not ghosts. They are entities that have chosen a life in darkness, deceit, and chaos. They have one intent in mind and that is to cause fear. Causing fear gives them the power they want over you.

Definition of demons:

"Demon" has a number of meanings, all related to the idea of a spirit that inhabited a place, or that accompanied a person. Whether such a dae-mon was benevolent or malevolent, the Greek word meant something different from the later medieval notions of 'demon', and scholars de-bate the time in which first century usage by Jews and Christians in its original Greek sense became transformed to the later medieval sense. Some de-nominations asserting Christian faith also include, exclusively or otherwise, fallen angels as de facto demons; this definition also covers the "sons of God" described in Genesis who abandoned their posts in heaven to mate with human women on Earth before the Deluge.

In the Gospel of Mark, Jesus casts out many de-mons, or evil spirits, from those who are afflicted with various ailments. Jesus is far superior to the power of demons over the beings that they in-habit, and he is able to free these victims by com-manding and casting out the demons, by binding them, and forbidding them to return. Jesus also lends this power to some of his disciples, who rejoice at their new found ability to cast out all de-mons. The demons are cast out by the pronuncia-tion of a name according to Matthew 7:22, some groups insisting the original pronunciation of the name Jesus and pure form of worship be used i.e. Yahshua / Joshua meaning "Yahweh is salvation".

By way of contrast, in the book of Acts a group

of Judaistic exorcists known as the sons of Sceva try to cast out a very powerful spirit without believing in or knowing Jesus, but fail with disastrous consequences. However Jesus himself never fails to vanquish a demon, no matter how powerful (see the account of the demon-possessed man at Gerasim), and even defeats Satan in the wilderness (see Gospel of Matthew).

There is a description in the Book of Revelation 12:7-17 of a battle between God's army and Satan's followers, and their subsequent expulsion from Heaven to Earth to persecute humans — although this event is related as being foretold and taking place in the future. In Luke 10:18 it is mentioned that a power granted by Jesus to cast out demons made Satan "fall like lightning from heaven."

Augustine of Hippo's reading of Apuleius, in City of God (Bk. IX, ch.11) is ambiguous as to whether daemons had become 'demonized' by the early 5th century:

He [Apulieus] also states that the blessed are called in Greek eudaimones, because they are good souls, that is to say, good demons, confirming his opinion that the souls of men are demons.

The contemporary Roman Catholic Church un-

15

equivocally teaches that angels and demons are real personal beings, not just symbolic devices. The Catholic Church has a cadre of officially sanctioned exorcists which perform many exorcisms each year. The exorcists of the Catholic Church teach that demons attack humans continually but that afflicted persons can be effectively healed and protected either by the formal rite of exorcism, authorized to be performed only by bishops and those they designate, or by prayers of deliverance which any Christian can offer for themselves or others.

Others

I will not be covering all elemental life in this book. I am only covering the three main causes of haunting and disruption.

To think that we are the only living beings in all the universes that exist is silly. Sometimes the lives of these other beings will interact with our own lives. I will not go into great detail about this subject here. I am just skimming the surface on this now because I have had clients come to me with this phenomenon and my own experiences with this subject and the importance of this will be brought up later on.

Definition of extraterrestrial life:

Various controversial claims have been made for evidence of extraterrestrial life. A less direct argument for the existence of extraterrestrial life relies on the vast size of the observable Universe. According to this argument, supported by scientists such as Carl Sagan and Stephen Hawking, it would be improbable for life not to exist somewhere other than Earth.

One possibility is that life has emerged independently at many places throughout the Universe. Another possibility is panspermia or exogenesis, in which life would have spread between habitable planets. These two hypotheses are not necessarily mutually exclusive.

Suggested locations at which life might have developed, or which might continue to host life today, include the planets Venus and Mars; moons of Jupiter, such as Europa; moons of Saturn, such as Titan and Enceladus; and extrasolar planets, such as Gliese 581 c, g and d, recently discovered to be near Earth mass and apparently located in their star's habitable zone, with the potential to have liquid water. In May 2011, NASA scientists reported that Enceladus "is emerging as the most habitable spot beyond Earth in the Solar System for life as we know it".

Beliefs that some unidentified flying objects are

of extraterrestrial origin, along with claims of alien abduction, are dismissed by most scientists. Most UFO sightings are explained either as sightings of Earth-based aircraft or known astronomical objects, or as hoaxes.

The Fine Line

Ghost, demons and extraterrestrial life are all related. Are they the same? No, but they do have similarities, making the removal process the same.

What they have in common:

1. They all answer to a higher power (god, the source, our father).

2. The ability to materialize and the ability to be invisible to the human eye.

3. Their fascination and interest in human life.

Discernment

How to know the good from the bad.

Common sense will serve you in discernment. General rules to follow:

1. How does it make you feel? Really stop and observe your feelings.

2. Does it cause fear or happy feelings?

3. Does it cause you confusion and indecision or clarity and comfort?

The answers to these questions will give you a good idea of what you are dealing with. Any negative thoughts and feelings is most definitely not good.

Keep in mind that even though you feel that the presence is a relative does not mean that it really is or that it is good. Trickery is used often by lower energy demons and ghosts especially right after someone passes on. Use your common sense in ALL matters.

CHAPTER 2

Personal
Encounters
with the
Unseen

Encounters

A few of my encounters.

Footsteps

It was a long and cold winter in the panhandle of Texas. The temperatures dipped down to negative 40 degrees in the early morning hours. I was very pregnant and due to give birth to my first child in 30 days. I had to walk everywhere I needed to go as I did not have a vehicle at that time.

I lived in an old house dated early 1900's, and I mean early. The house was so old that the wood that was the walls had shrunk and in some parts of the house and you could see right outside. Yes, no insulation just wood for walls. It was terrible but the rent was very reasonable at $80 per month.

I know, it sounds like one of those old timer stories (uphill barefoot, in the snow) but it isn't. It was real.

I lived there with my husband, the father of the child I was carrying and a new white puppy which plays a significant part in this encounter.

I had to make a trip to the store for supplies so I bundled up with two pairs of pants, three shirts and a jacket that would not button around my pregnant belly. I made it there and back a little frozen but fine. The day was like any other day. My husband worked that day so I was home alone with my new puppy and the mice that had taken up residency in the kitchen.

Evening came and my husband arrived home. We had dinner, watched some television and then retired for the evening around 10pm. My husband did not like the puppy to stay in the house so I was forced to take the puppy outside to his dog house before retiring. The dog house sat in the front yard of the house.

I leashed the puppy to his dog house and made sure that his blankets were setup properly then I returned to the house and went to bed.

I was awoke around 2am, I could hear all the dogs in the neighborhood barking in a very panicked and frightened manner. My first thought was what was causing the fear and what wild animal may be out there. I was frightened for my puppy so I got up and went out side. I looked up and down the street and could see nothing. The neighborhood dogs continued to bark. I checked on the puppy and he seemed a bit shaken. I could not leave him outside like that so I prompted him to follow me inside the house. He trailed behind me up the front porch steps and into the house.

I closed and locked the front door and proceeded to the restroom. The puppy was right on my heels the whole way. I sat on the commode and the puppy sat on the floor next to me. I looked at the puppy when suddenly the puppy cocked his head as if he was listening to something. Suddenly there was loud footsteps going down the hallway, it sounded like someone with cowboy boots and spurs. The dog was still listening with his head cocked. He seemed confused. I was scared out of my mind. I thought someone broke in. I ran to the bedroom to wake my husband. He got up and armed himself. He went through the whole house and found nothing. All the doors were locked, no one was there.

It was hard getting back to sleep after that. I did not sleep much that night. The following weeks came with more footsteps and a man calling my name. Even my husband was scared because he also heard the footsteps and the voice.

We could not move out right away so we took the front room which was the living room and stayed only in there. The rest of the house was abandoned by us.

Desert Chills

While living in Las Vegas for a couple of years

trips out to the desert were common for stargazing and recreation.

It was a clear and warm night with a slight breeze. My boyfriend and I along with his bull terrier were on our way to a remote part of the desert outside the city limits of Las Vegas to do some star gazing. We packed up the van with our supplies and headed out.

We took our usual route out into the desert. We turned off onto a dirt forest service road. Everything seemed fine for a mile or so. I should mention that from years of experience I have learned to always pay attention to your pets and their reactions as they are more in tune with the unseen than most people.

My boyfriend was driving and I was seated in the back near the dog when all of a sudden the hairs on the dogs back stood straight up on end and he became very alert. After about 20 seconds the dog let out a low growl. We were still driving down the road at this point. I watched the dog closely. My boyfriend stopped the van and got out to look if someone was out there. There was no one out there. Suddenly the dog went into a violent barking and growling frenzy towards the front of the van. I did not see anything. My boyfriend got spooked and jumped back in the van. Suddenly a rush of intense energy went right through me. My eyes began to well up, I had a knot in my throat, and I was shaking. I screamed " turn around and get out of here now !", "something is here and it is not good !"

He turned the van around and we sped out of there. We came to the paved road and he pulled to the side to make sure we were alright. Not even 10 seconds after we stopped that same rush of energy filled the van and again I told him to go. The intense energy continued to follow us but it became weaker the closer we got to home.

Residual energy was around for a couple weeks but it was not as intense as the area where we first encountered the energy.

Being Chased

I felt like I would never be left a lone and I was desperate for help during this time. I was similar to a newborn as I was not educated very well on what was happening in my life. During this time I bought book after book with still no answer as to why this was happening. Not knowing and not understanding these things can cause fear, real fear. The turning point came much later in my life during the passing of my mother which I will get back to later.

The following incident was an ongoing theme in my life. It is by no accident that this happens. When you are sensitive to the unseen they just know.

I was living in Miami with my children and a friend. We lived in an older home, built around the early 1920's. I did not think too much about it at the time.

After living there about a week I started to see dark energy in the hallway. Specifically an area that led to the attic. I was not the only one that was seeing it, my daughter was seeing it as well. It disturbed her sleep on several occasions.

One night when it was just me and the children I felt the presence stronger than usual. It was an over powering negative energy. I heard a noise out in the back yard and went out to see what it was. I walked out to the front yard and around through the back gate. As I looked I saw a mass of dark energy approaching me in the back yard, I was terrified. I turned to leave when all of a sudden it sped up towards me. I ran to the house and all the while it was right behind me. I made it to the front door and ran into the house slamming the door behind me. I went to the kitchen and hid under the dining room table. I sat there for a while not knowing what to do.

The front door opened and it was my friend. I felt relieved.

The haunting was on going and only intensified from this point causing fear with my children and self.

Knock at The Door

This happened at the same house I spoke of in the previous story.

It was a normal sunny day in Miami. I took the children to the beach, relaxed with a book, had dinner, watched television and went to bed. I did not have any trouble falling a sleep and slept very well until I was awoken at 2:00am with a slow and subtle knock, knock, knock at the door. It would pause in between the three knocks for a moment as if someone was at the door waiting for some-one to answer. I listened again and again three knocks at the front door. I gathered myself and rolled out of bed. I could feel the cold bare floor on my feet as I walked to the front door. I did not turn on any lights because I wanted to see who it was before I made them aware someone was coming to the door. I quietly went to the door and stood on the tips of my toes to see out the peep hole.

As I looked I saw a young girl about age 7 standing at the door. I looked again to be sure and when I looked again I noticed she was wearing clothing from the late 1800's. Again, three knocks as I stood there by the door. My instincts told me not to open the door. I looked out the peep hole again but this time the little girl was looking up at me and the peep hole. I was spooked. I looked again and she was gone.

Screams in The Woods

After leaving Miami we went north to the panhandle of Florida where we lived for about a year. As always after a move things would be quiet for a few weeks to a month. I always felt like I was being followed by these ghosts and it took them that long to find me. In reality after a move it usually takes that long for your presence to be noticed by the unseen in the area that you moved to. Time is not a factor in the unseen world, what seems like a month to us is merely a blink of an eye to them.

We lived in a home that was situated a block from the ocean with a canal running along side it. It was nice and secluded. The nearest neighbor was a couple acres away. Pine trees lined the yard and provided abundant shade and wildlife. The area where the canal was is where most of the nightly activity would be. I am not referring to wildlife, I am referring to unseen visitors.

For weeks I would hear the sounds of a woman screaming. This would happen between the hours of 1:00 am and 3:00 am almost every morning. No one was out there because I did check into it the first few times it would happen. The woman was screaming as if she was hurt or being hurt, it was a shrilling scream. Along with the screams I would hear children playing along the canal.

It was 2:00 am and someone was beating on my door in a panic. Not just knocking but literally beating on the door. I woke up and went to the door. I asked who it was through the door. A woman replied "I need help". I opened the door and let her in. She claimed to have just left the bar down the road (of which there was not one). She made me very uneasy. There was something about her that was way off. She sat for a while telling me how she was lost and needed to get home. I told her she could get help from my neighbor but she refused to go there. Actually she was quite livid about going over there. I went to the neighbors to get her help. After I returned she decided to go to the neighbors. I never saw her again after that. Note: Sometimes the unseen are able to manifest into physical form and this was a good example of one such occurrence.

Why? The time this happened, her resistance to go for help, coupled with her strange behavior leads me to believe this was not an actual person.

Unexpected Abilities

A friend of mine had been talking extensively with me about meditation, remote viewing and channeling. At this time in my life I did not know anything about these topics, at least not by these titles. I was curious.

Due to my keen sensitivity and awareness my friend suggested that I try meditation. I agreed, so we setup a time and place for the meditation. On that day late in the evening my friend directed me to meditate by laying on a floor cushion in an isolated room where I would not be disturbed. He did not direct me on what to meditate on or what to do when meditating, he merely told me to just to relax and look within myself.

I laid on the cushion that was there on the floor in the middle of the room, I took deep cleansing breaths and relaxed. Within 5 minutes I was in a deep meditative state. I saw cities, lights, and people. As I continued I saw a couple in their late 50's sitting at a dinning table talking about their trip. They had taken their boat out that day. They were drinking tea from decorative tea cups. I saw the room they were in and what they were wearing, every detail was as clear as if I was actually there in the room myself.

I was deep in meditation and viewing what was going on with this couple when I was tapped on my shoulder by my friend. He said that it had been an hour and he thought I fell asleep instead of meditating so he thought he would wake me up.

I sat up feeling a bit light headed. I paused for a moment or two then got up from the cushion. We went to the other room and I told him everything that I saw. He was shocked and amazed. He told me I was describing his parents perfectly. He was so excited that he had to call his parents to see what they were doing right that minute. He wanted to confirm they were who I was seeing. He confirmed it right down to what they were wearing.

Keep in mind that I have never met my friends parents at that time. They lived in Miami and I was living in Las Vegas at the time.

Through meditation I had tapped into a part of myself that was laying dormant. This meditation opened me up to many other abilities that were dormant for years.

Tall Visitor

I loved living in the country because of the peace and quiet but it was anything but quiet. It was not the neighbors that were noisy, it was the unseen forces that frequented the area that caused such a ruckus.

There are several encounters here. I wanted to put them all together since they are related to my time in this area. I lived there with my children. They were ages 12, 8, 4 at the time.

I lived there for about a year and what a year it was. I became friends with a couple of the neighbors down the road because my children were friends with their children.

The curious family down the road was always talking about their lights going on and off all by themselves and hearing strange noises when no one was there. I thought it was interesting and went on with raising my children. At that time I was dealing with my own ghosts. These ghosts had a habit of appearing again within two months of me moving. It was like it took them that long to find me again.

After about three month's of living there I first noticed the behavior of my youngest child. He was out of character. He was very unruly, even for him. It was like he was being influenced by something. One day was worse than the rest of the days, he just threw a huge fit. I dealt with it through prayer, meditation and positive energy. This child had nightmares almost every night so he needed me to be there so he could fall asleep. He would have the same nightmares about small men taking him places. This is another topic for another book.

That same night everyone was restless. Even I could not fall asleep. With my children asleep in their rooms I began to doze off when all of a sudden a heavy pressure was on top of me, I was paralyzed and could not get up. The pressure became more intense the more I struggled to get up. I called out for help but no one came. I was on my own so I prayed and asked for help. I saw my oldest child walk into my room with a blank look on his face. He turned and left my room and as he did the pressure was gone and I called my sons name but he did not respond so I got up to check on him. When I got to the doorway of his room I noticed he was fast asleep as if he never got up and never came to my room.

The next morning I asked him about it and he said that he never got up. I was determined to find out what was going on so I contacted several psychics for advice. All this happened early on in my experiences and I was not very knowledgeable at this time. One psychic was a big help to me and suggested nightlights to ward of the negative energies. She also told me that I had quite a following. She proceeded to tell me about all the spirits that follow me every day. She said I had the gift of spirit communication and that they are drawn to me because of this. I thought to myself "great, just what I need". I was being sarcastic of course.

I did what she had advised and it seemed to help somewhat. The haunting in that house got so bad that we all slept (me and my children) on the living room floor together. Night after night was the same. I prayed and meditated and asked for help over and over. I was in tears at this point, I cried myself to sleep that night.

It was 2:00 am and I was awoken by a sense of something being in the room. It was not a frightful feeling, but it was a calm, peaceful feeling. The energy filled the room. I sat up and looked past my feet to see a tall white robed figure standing there. He stood all the way to the ceiling of the room. I felt safe and cared for. The robed figure spoke to me and told me that it would be alright, that I would make it through all this and that they have been watching over me. I noticed his stature, white robe and large eyes then I fell back to sleep.

Best night's sleep I had in months.

Son's Night Terrors

My youngest son was having trouble sleeping. The source of his night terrors was very disturbing. I thought it had to do with the frequently unseen visitors to our home but I was wrong.

Even after he would fall asleep he would wake up most nights screaming. He would say things like "they were there", "They are coming to get me". I would have to stay with him all night to keep the night terrors away.

When he was old enough (4 years old) to draw and I could understand him better, he drew me a picture of what was bothering him at night. I was shocked and at a loss for words.

My son drew these small figures, he said there was a few of them and they would force him to go with them at night. They were about 4 feet tall, large heads and large eyes and a thin body. I knew I had seen this somewhere before so I began my research.

What he described are classified as "Greys".

Grey aliens (or "Greys") are alleged extraterrestrial beings whose existence is promoted in ufological, paranormal, and New Age communities, named for their skin color.

Paranormal and pseudoscientific claims involving Greys vary in every respect including their nature (ETs, extradimensionals, demons, or machines), origins, moral dispositions, intentions, and physical appearances (even +varying in their eponymous skin color). A composite description derived from overlap in claims would have Greys as small bodied, sexless beings with smooth grey skin, enlarged head and large eyes. The origin of the idea of the Grey is commonly associated with the Betty and Barney Hill abduction claim, although skeptics see precursors in science fiction and earlier paranormal claims.

Through my research I found this to be a common occurrence in children. Since this incident with my son I have had a few clients come to me with this situation.

Granddaughter Waving

It was a cool winter evening and I was watching my granddaughters so my daughter could go out for the evening. We watched some television, played with toys and had an evening snack.

I decided to go outside to see the full moon

and gaze at the stars. One of my granddaughters wanted to come outside with me so she followed me out the front door to the porch.

We had a seat in one of the chairs. My granddaughter sat on my lap. Next to the front porch was the carport and then the long driveway. We talked about the stars and the moon, she loved the moon.

My granddaughter became distracted. She lifted her hand and waved toward the carport. I looked to see if someone was there but I saw no one. She waved again but this time after she waved she became shy by putting her face in my shoulder. I still did not see anyone.

I asked her who she was waving at and she said she was not allowed to tell. I was concerned and we went inside the house. I never found out who she was waving at but I can say that since then my daughter has had a few unseen visitors.

The Old Corner Saloon

For whatever reason my Father was compelled to buy an old rundown saloon that was established in the 1800's. Keep in mind that my parents did not believe that ghosts were real. They felt they were all made up, a hallucination. I kept away from the subject with them because of this.

I was looking at pictures of the saloon after he purchased the saloon. I saw several pictures of ghosts in the photos. I showed my parents but they insisted it was just shadow. I knew better. I thought, "this is going to be fun" sarcastically.

My Parents settled in and opened the saloon for business. I helped out a few nights during the week.

My mother was very artistic and setup her studio in a room with its own entrance on the side of the saloon. She would come into the saloon on her breaks and my Father would prepare her lunch.

I did most of the closings at the saloon for my parents. One night my parents decided to close the saloon themselves so I stayed home.

The very next day my parents were anxious to talk with me. My mother told me how they heard footsteps on the wood floor and then something grabbed her shoulder from behind. I knew the place was haunted but I kept it to myself.

My parents never got over the incident, they were telling everyone that would listen. From that time on they were believers in the existence of ghosts and I became the go to person.

All Hell Broke Loose

In 1995 I lived in Sedona Arizona and it had been 5 years since I spoke with either of my parents. We had a falling out and I felt this was the best way for me to deal with the situation.

I worked during the day at a local restaurant and on some days I volunteered at "The Center For The New Age". Every day I kept hearing this little voice inside me saying "you need to go to your parents, it may be the last time you will see them". Of course like most of us, I ignored the inner promptings for a while till it became so loud that it was annoying. I decided to move back to California to be next to them.

It took a couple weeks to find a house and to get settled in. My parents seemed fine for those two weeks. However I did notice my Mother's eyes were not very clear. I asked her if she was alright and she always replied "I am fine".

It had been two months since I moved back to California and on one visit to see my Mother I noticed she would not sit down and her eyes appeared to have a film over them. I asked her and she said she was having a problem with her tail bone and that her other bones also ached. She was also having a problem with her mouth and gums. I urged her to go to the Doctor but she was always very stubborn and refused. Another month passed and I could see her health was deteriorating.

I received a phone call from my Dad, he was panicked. He took my Mother to the Emergency Room and he called to let me know. I gathered my things and got a sitter for the kids and went to the hospital. When I got there my Dad was standing outside the exam room where my Mother was. He said he had to call everyone else and asked if I would go in and stay with my Mother till he got back. I entered the room and the Doctor followed in behind me. As I stood there beside her the Doctor told her she had Myeloid Leukemia and that it was to far advanced to treat. My Mother broke down crying, I comforted her and cried with her. My Dad walked in and I told him the diagnosis, he was frantic. He did not know how to deal with the news so he left the room to make phone calls to the family. I stayed with my Mother and she soon settled down.

My Mother was admitted to the hospital and moved to a private room. Hospice was called later that day because my Mother wanted to be at home. The next day my Mother was driven home by my Dad.

Family started to arrive at my parents home. My three sisters and my brother were there. Hospice provided a nurse that came twice a day to administer pain medication and for my Mothers other medical needs.

A couple days passed and during those days my Mother was coherent. On the third day she was in and out of consciousness and was between two worlds (that is what I call it). She was not making any sense at this point. She would be talking to someone that was not there and she was telling me about the litter along side the road. She was as sweet as could be to me but was very angry with my older sister and at one point told her to go away. It made no sense because my older sister was always her favorite. She was between worlds all day.

Later that night I was outside and suddenly I heard a voice that said "she will pass tonight". I quickly told the family not to go to sleep as our Mother will pass tonight. They questioned me and I told them that was what I know. They listened to what I said and we stayed by our Mothers side.

At 2:00 am my Dad screamed, we ran in the

house to find our Mother not breathing. We stood over her when suddenly she grasped her last breath and passed away.

During the three days before our Mother passed away there was a lot of talk about the other side with my sisters claiming they had seen something in the house and outside the window of the house where our Mother was resting. My sisters claim they were angels but I had other feelings on that.

After my mother was picked up by the funeral home I went home. As I drove into the driveway my oldest son ran out of the house screaming "grandma is dead and she is in my room". My son was frantic and insisted I go to his room now. I went into his room and nothing was there. He told me how her head was floating in the corner of his room. Kinda creepy. It took me an hour to get the kids calmed down. They finally realized how tired they were and fell asleep.

The next day me and my siblings were to meet with our Dad to make the final arrangements. I got up around 8am, had my coffee and went to take a shower. After my shower I heard my Mothers voice. She was asking me what had happened to her. She then appeared to me and followed me around the house asking questions. This was nothing new to me at this point in my life as I had seen many ghosts and I was very well educated in the afterlife.

My Mother came with me to my Dads house and continued to ask questions. I explained the situation to her but she kept insisting that she was alive and wanted to know why no one else could hear her.

Three days past and my Mother was no longer around in spirit form, at least I was not hearing or seeing her but the terror was about to begin.

I was in the living area of my home with my kids and a friend, it was around 7pm. I got up from the couch and started towards the kitchen. I went no more than two steps when all of a sudden a rush of cold energy drove right through me. I felt a very strong presence that caused my eyes to water, my throat to become restricted and my body to shake. I called to my friend because I was unable to move. My friend and my oldest son came into the room. My son panicked and lifted me off the floor and onto the couch making sure my feet were not touching the ground. The symptoms began to subside. I asked my son why he lifted me to the couch and he said " I saw a dark shadow on the floor moving toward you", "I was afraid it was going to move into you".

Later that same night my kids were unable to sleep because of a voice calling to them (they said it was my Mother) and the smell of my Mothers perfume lingered in their room.

Several days would pass without an incident after I would pray and meditate asking for protection. I decided to go inward to see where my Mother was in the afterlife. I found her in a dimly lit place which I call the midway point. It is a place for souls that do not know what has happened to them, a place where souls go to sort things out. They are kept isolated from each other. The only time they become aware of where they are and the others around them is when they wake up and realize what has happened to them. In this place there is unending space and many areas for souls, sort of like rooms with no doors. The Archangels are there watching over the souls. No help is given unless asked for. Imagine a huge space and as you look down you see the rooms with no doors, each space is secluded from the next. There was no way to contact her while she was in this space so I prayed to give her help.

Knowing where my Mother was ruled out her being the one that was visiting us. It was something else, something that was taking full advantage of the grief that we were feeling.

It was daytime and I was driving to the local store when an ugly being appeared beside me in the passenger seat of my car and began clawing at me with long finger nails. I pulled over and asked for help in prayer out loud causing it to leave.

I had enough and headed to a local church for help. I spoke with two pastors and they took me to the back to anoint me with oil and pray over me. They told me that sometimes a family can have attachments from the past. They felt that was the cause of the harassment. I left the church feeling like maybe it will stop now.

It was fine for a few days and then started up again, this time it was worse. I knew I would have to face it head on and take care of it myself. I read many books and tried many different techniques and most only helped for a short time. I prayed and meditated and received my help. I unlocked the part of myself that knew what to do.

I proceeded with my three step process and cleared my home, my children and myself. I have not had a haunting this big since. Now they tend to walk a mile around me just to avoid me.

Water Logged

When I lived in a rural area where the river ran

just 50 feet from my home it seemed peaceful. It always is when you first move in. There were empty homes around me waiting for the right tenant.

A couple months later a new tenant was moving in right next to me. It was a spiritual man that had a strange feel about him, I could not quite put my finger on it but I knew he was hiding something from his past.

He told me that he had lived here about 10 years ago and that it was good to be back home.

After about a week I began to feel uneasy about my new neighbor. I had to add thick covers to my windows to block out energy coming from his direction into my home. I had a few restless nights because of it.

A month had past and I was attempting to get some sleep when I heard a noise, I got up and went into the living room and there stood a girl in her twenties, soaking wet with water falling off of her onto my carpet. Her head was tilted (her neck appeared broken) and her skin was a bluish color. I knew it was a ghost but why was she here?

Suddenly the ghost fed me information. She was killed by the man that lived behind me and the man was recently out of prison for the incident. It all finally made sense. Goes to show you, you never really know who your neighbors are.

CHAPTER 3

Client

Questions

&

Answers

Questions and Answers

Client encounters.

Heavy Footsteps

Question

When I'm off to bed, turn off the lights. I feel like there is someone lying next to me and I hear deep breathing sounds and when I turn the lights back on and I don't hear anything and this repeats the entire night till I ignore it and sleep. My sister have heard very heavy footsteps.(me and my sister have separate rooms and this only happens on the top floor)Is this some sort of paranormal activity? If yes, is there a way out? Thanks

Answer

Yes, you have a ghost. If your home is older or has a history it may be attached to the house. You can perform a house clearing by using incense or a sage stick and burning it in the house. Take the lit incense and walk through the house making sure to reach all corners, doorways and windows, this may need to be repeated for several days. If that does not work you may have a stubborn ghost that does not want to leave in which case you can express your want for the ghost to leave just by telling it to leave. Same as you would tell a live person that you did not want in your home. Always remember not to express fear in any way. State your position firmly.

If you still have problems you may need a professional to clear your home.

Ghost Biting

Question

My girlfriend recently experience a very paranormal incident and would like your help. A month ago, my girlfriend answered to a call in her hostel bathroom only to find out that there was no one there calling for her. After the answering, she has been receiving this unexplained paranormal biting all around her body. Though it's not pain, you could find bite mark (with teeth marking) all around her body - neck, back, thigh, hand, everywhere, except her face. Her roommate that is in the same room as her could not explain it as the mark only appears the next morning.

We would like to know what causes this problem. Is it that they are looking for our help? Though frighten, my girlfriend would like to know the reason for this paranormal activity.

Maybe you could advise us on this.

Thanks so much.

Answer

Here are a few reasons why ghosts bite.

A Ghosts of any age sometimes bite to get attention. When real ghosts are in situations where they are not receiving enough positive attention and daily interaction, they often find a way to make others sit up and take notice. Biting is a quick way to become the center of attention, even if it is negative attention.

IMITATION - Many ghosts do love to imitate others. Watching others and trying to let them know they are around they show their presence to a haunted location. Sometimes as we all do ghosts see others bite and decide to try it out themselves to see if they can effect the living.

TERITORY - Some believe that real ghosts are trying so hard to show possession of a location. Learning to do things independently, making choices, and needing control over a situation are part of a haunting. Biting is a powerful way to control others.

FRUSTRATION - You have to realize that a ghost as being what it is experience a lot of frustration. Being Dead is a real struggle. D consider this when they can't find away to make people hear their words to express their feelings, they resort to hitting, pushing, or biting.

STRESS - A lack of daily routine, interesting things to do, or interaction with loved one's or just another human being are stressful situations for the dead. When a person transits to the other side they also experience stressful events of what they see family members going through. Biting is one way to express feelings and relieve tension. It is also a way to show persons that you do not like what they are doing.

You may want to look into your location as this may be a ghost from some time ago. I would suggest clearing the building using incense or a sage stick. Light the incense or sage stick and walk through the building with it making sure to reach all corners, doors and windows. After the incense you can also place natural quartz crystals (size does not matter) in the area, one for each corner of the building or room, this will create a grid. For self protection visualize a sphere of white light around yourself before bedtime and this can be reinforced by wearing a quartz crystal or placing one under your pillow.

Amelia Earhart

Question

A few years ago, I discovered I had the ability to communicate with the dead and have been very careful with this gift. I communicate with a spirit guardian. Through her, I channeled Amelia Earhart and we have become very close and communicate daily. We have communicated with each other for the last three years. I can "sense" her around me and say something to her and she will reply by moving my arm in a direction that she and I have agreed upon. My question, is why she would be there at the right time when I channeled her. And I know it's her, as I have read two biographies on her and she exhibits her personality. Can you help me out with this question? Thanks.

Answer

It is your intention to speak with her and the knowledge you are ready for now that brings her to you at this time. The transfer of energy is great.

Black Shadow

Question

My daughter recently started having nightmares about someone trying to take her and she said she also saw snakes. She wakes up several times at night and at times I would notice that she would see something then she would squeeze me and say she was scared but at that time would not tell me she was seeing anything. I then started having nightmares about something doing harm to my child but I could not see what it was. She just recently told me she sees a shadow come in to the room when she is sleeping and also sees it go in and out of the walls by the restroom and the closet both upstairs in our bedroom where me and her sleep. My brother in law then told me he has seen this shadow go upstairs and stand by the stair case then disappear. I have never seen it and I am worried about it because my daughter is very afraid to be alone upstairs. She also said that when she would have bad dreams she would pray and they would go away but now even praying is not helping and she still has bad dreams and continues to see this shadow. She said it has no shape its just a black shadow that moves across the room or hovers above her like on the clings. What could this be and how do I get it to go away?

Answer

You have a lower level entity that is bothering your child. It is a lower entity that likes to cause fear. It is not uncommon for children to see and feel these lower level entities.

Here are a few things you can do

Clear the child's space by burning a sage stick or some incense. Carry the incense or sage stick with you through the house especially the child's room while repeating "all lower and negative energies be gone, only the highest light energy shall remain".

Reinforce the clearing by adding nightlights to the area of concern.

Teach your child to place a bubble of white light around themselves (visually thinking it to be there) before going to sleep.

If this does not work for you then let me know and I will do a remote clearing.

Gates of Hell

Question

Saturday January 16th at around am me and 8 other people were playing with a Ouija board, we got all 8 people to go with it and had a spirit come to us. At first it said it was from the sun, supposedly meaning good and then it later said it was from the moon, we talked with it for around 10 minutes in 3 or 4 different sessions, we asked its name and it spelled out Esther we asked its last name it spelled out Carlson, we asked it if it was hurt it answered yes, we asked if it had done something wrong it answered yes, we asked it if it was trapped in the fiery gates of hell it answered yes, we asked how old it was it just went on 8, we looked the person up on Google and found that an Esther Carlson died when she was 88, she was a murderer and had killed her husband.

That day we had a funeral for a kid who used to go to school with us but moved when he was in 3rd grade he had committed suicide and most of our grade took it hard, one friend who had also went to the funeral with me took it really hard and someone said something about the person and my friend got extremely upset and after that felt really sick and couldn't stop shaking.

My question is, do you think Esther Carlson could be possessing him? If you need more information just e-mail me and I can tell you what ever you need to know.

Answer

Some signs of the beginning of possession include shaking, lump in throat, illness and tension. Yes it sounds like an attempt or successful possession. How is your friend now? Are there any changes in their personality? Or appearance? Habits?

Most likely the spirit you encountered through the Ouija board is lying to you. Whenever you use a Ouija board you open doorways to lower entities, lower demonic beings. I suggest you hold a gathering with the same people and close the doorway(s). Just gather in the same manner and call in the higher beings of light and request assistance in closing all doorways that were opened. If the doorway(s) are left open it could cause you further problems.

Follow-up Question

Well that night he did get sick and shaking I was standing by him and he was trembling horribly. Now he said he cannot sleep, he shakes every time someone comes by him and he feels different. And does he need to be there for the closing of the doorways? And what do we all have to do? Is that it or do you think he may need a total exorcism, which I have heard are not done by the church as much any more.

Answer

If you gather together in the same place and form a circle then ask the higher light beings (God, Holy spirit, Archangels, whichever you prefer) and together as one voice make the request to close the doorway(s), ask to clear and remove all negative and lower energies from your friend. Ask that all that has passed through the doorway(s) to be returned from where they came. Repeat several times. Close your session by giving thanks for the assistance.

This should work as long as all of you stay focused. If for some reason it does not work you may need to get local help for your friend.

Some churches do still provide help.

Follow-up Question

I saw him today he looks fine and was just quiet... And he talked with a friend who bought the Ouija board and he said she cannot talk to him that he gets sick when she does because of the Ouija board... So I think we are going to go through with what you told me. So do we need to do anything with the Ouija board? And does the one we think is possessed need to be there?

Answer

Yes, everyone needs to be there. Even the one you think is possessed.

Deja Vu

Question

There are sometimes when I feel that what is happening around me has happened before. Like I have seen it in my dreams, months back. How is this possible?

Answer

It is called deja vu. Where you will have memories of an instance that has already occurred. It is a time when you are in sync and alignment with your spiritual self. Your spiritual self lives a step ahead and knows what is going to occur before your physical self does. When alignment occurs you receive memories before they happen.

If you want to read more on this topic there are many articles online, just search deja vu.

Shadow Men

Question

I have been attacked by "shadow men" both physically and mentally. They have tried to posses me twice, but failed. Is this because I have the holy spirit?

Answer

Yes. Whenever you are drawing light to yourself (holy spirit, god) you will get noticed and challenged until you learn how to protect yourself. The best thing to do is to intend a light of protection around yourself and your surroundings. Even a deep cleansing of your home will help.

Most people do not notice these attacks so I believe that you are more aware than most which is good, but this also has it's disadvantages.

Haunted Land

Question

My son is 8 years old. For the past 3 years, he has said he hears noises at night. He can't see the noise, but only hear it. He hears it every night about 3 am It only happens when everyone in the house is sleeping. He has been very descriptive. He has said that it sounds like someone is walking down the hall wearing wind pants. The noise always walks around his bed. It touches his feet. He said a couple times that it sounds like the person ("noise") was standing next to his bed with a plastic bag and a book, and was going to put the book in the bag. He is so scared at night that he has to have his radio really loud to avoid hearing the noise. He puts two pillows at the foot of his bed with thick fleece blankets on top of the pillows - just so he doesn't feel the noise touch his feet. He has a night lamp and a night light on every night. His curtains have to be open. His closet doors have to be shut. His bedroom door has to be open. We have done numerous things to help reassure him that he is safe. We have walked through the house to show him there is nothing in our house that will hurt him. He says he can't see the noise so walking through the house doesn't help. We have read books about God. He has told the noise to leave him alone. He's said a prayer to God. He has an Indian dream catcher next to his door as well as a cross, but he still hears the noise. We had our house blessed by our Father a week ago. After that, my son said he doesn't understand why he still hears the noise because the noise should be gone now that our house is blessed. He said the noise is worse now and he thinks the devil is in our house. A little background ... we built our house 3 years ago. We had a puppy who died for unknown reasons 2 years ago. We now have a new puppy. We live on the outskirts of town so I wonder if something maybe happened on this land. I don't know if the noise could be our dead puppy's spirits because it won't leave and it always walks around my son's bed. My son and puppy were pretty close so it was devastating when our puppy passed away. We do not know what to do. Our son is awake every night from approximately 3 am to 5 am due to the noise. I wake every morning to my son sleeping on my bedroom floor. I want him to feel safe and secure in his bedroom but I don't foresee that happening any time soon. Do you have any suggestions of what we can do to help him? Your help will be GREATLY appreciated!!!!!

Answer

The Father that blessed the house may not have had the experience or belief to get the job done. Of course the spirit is mad now because you are attempting to remove it. You can assure your son that it is not the devil. It may want you to believe that but it is not. It is not the puppy that has passed away.

It is a spirit that is intent on creating fear in your son. I am not going to go into great detail on the spirit as this will just create attention.

You need to do the following for three days at the same time each night.

Take a white candle and light it and place it in the center of the room. Take either incense or a sage wand the light it now walk around the room making sure the smoke surrounds all areas your son refers to as being hot spots. While using the incense repeat "This space is free and clear of all lower entities and lower influences, only the highest light and love may enter this space". Do this for three nights at the same time. You may also add moth balls to each corner of the space. Another trick is to place salt around the perimeter or you may place natural quartz crystals in each corner of the room.

If you are not confident enough to carry this out it may not work. Approach this the same way you would if a person you did not want was in your house. Be firm and confident.

Deceased Mother

Question

My sister and I really need to get in contact with our mother, she has been dead for many years but we believe that her spirit is with us however we need some clearer communication.

Answer

The best time to contact the deceased is within the first month after they have passed. After this time most of the deceased have moved on into their new lives in other places/realms. Contacting your mother at this point may not provide any results unless she is an earth bound spirit. If you feel she is earth bound, contacting her will provide you with the results you seek.

Passed On

Question

My question is why am I feeling such strong emotions for, and an emotional connection to someone who has passed on, who I never even knew in life, but only knew of. I do not understand how I could be having these emotions for a person who had absolutely nothing to do with my life when alive? And why would he be affecting my life now that he is dead? I have also been having many different about him too.

I would appreciate any help.

Answer

Due to your perception and you being familiar, this ghost is reaching out to you in an attempt to feel alive.

It would be best to direct him to go into the light.

Empath

Question

Ever since I got into watching Star Trek TNG on rental I have been fascinated by the character Deanna Tori's abilities as a empath. Are there many like that, or do psychic mediums usually pretty much have that covered in their specialty?

Answer

There are empaths. Not all psychic mediums have this ability.

Follow-up Question

Do you by chance know how I could meet one such empaths? Or even a test I could take to see how well I do at knowing how people are feeling?

Answer

Empaths are private people and will not readily admit to such an ability. There are no tests for measuring this ability.

Ghost Calling

Question

I have a question I hope you can help me with. My dad died last august and since then he's been in my dreams three times. I never see him though. I just hear him.

The first two times was within a month's time after his death and in the dream he called me on the phone and said my name and because I knew he was dead, I got scarred and quickly hung up both times.

I did not have any more dreams after those 2 until yesterday. I was having a weird dream and all the sudden it changed and I heard his voice talking to me, but I couldn't make out everything he was saying, because he was always hard to understand when he was alive. All I heard was that something was split in two or something like that and then I woke up.

Is he trying to get a hold of me to tell me something? I have never been really close to him when he was alive or anything so there is not much of an emotional attachment for my end, even though I did care about him.

I would just like to know what possibly could be going on, because this type of dreams really freak me out and I'm hoping that he's not haunting me, because I couldn't afford a cemetery to place his ashes and they are at the bottom of my stairs in my apartment.

Thank you for your help.

Answer

Let him speak and see what he says the next

time you have the dream. It may be just something he wanted to tell you. Or you may feel guilty about something which is causing the dreams. From what you have told me I do not believe it is a haunting.

Negative Energy

Question

Is there negative energy around me or is there any in my home? I feel always down and I feel my house is sad. Thank you for you time. Hope to hear from you soon.

Answer

You actually answered the question for yourself. It may be time for a clearing of body, mind and soul. Feeling sad and/or down will attract more of the same to you and your home. If your feelings were sudden you may have an unwanted visitor or unwanted attachment.

Black Orb

Question

Is there such thing as an black orb if so what does it mean and how big is it ? Is it dangerous ? Can it harm anybody ?

Answer

Yes there are black orbs. It is composed of negative/lower energies and I would just leave it alone. The potential to cause harm is there but it really depends on the individual and the circumstances.

Pressure on Chest

Question

So here's the story. My friends parents were out of town and me and him decided to grab something to eat and eat at the kitchen table. Now all week we have noticed that his two cats have been acting weird, weird as in meowing for no reason, hiding, running. So anyway me and my friend are sitting at his kitchen table eating some fast food and I mentioned to him before that I thought I saw something but then again it could have been my imagination. We were eating and I hear a noise come from the hall by the upstairs, I look over to the hall and he goes "Hats wrong?" I said that I heard something and it sounded weird. All of a sudden he just stares at where I heard the noise and I ask him what wrong and he says "Oh my god!" I look and there's nothing there. He says

"Oh my god its right behind me!" Both of us felt a huge pressure, he held his chest and couldn't speak or breathe for at least 2 seconds. I almost passed out because I felt really light headed. I never saw him cry before and he literally burst into tears and said we have to get out of here. We both ran out of the house and talked over what happened when we went for a walk. He said he looked where I heard that weird noise and said he saw a dark figure with a hood pass by the hallway really slow. Then he said it felt like it sped up behind him and went into him and he couldn't breathe nor speak. He also said it felt like someone was pushing on his chest and he was being stabbed. Like I said I just felt like I was going to pass out, a really light headed feeling and my whole body was heavy. Anyways we were driving to my house to get away and he said "It wants me back, I need to go back." I couldn't believe was he just said and he said you have to hurry the force is getting stronger and he drove back to his house. He said as soon as he went home he turned off everything except a little light on the microwave and sat in his kitchen. His cats were nowhere to be seen and he couldn't find them. He said he froze and couldn't move. He texted me saying "Help I can't move I'm frozen I don't know why." He told me that it wanted him to stay there with him. He finally got up after twenty minutes and drove over to my house again. The next morning he found scratches on his arms with no explanation. We went back to the house and the cats were there. His closet door was open and he said he never goes in there. The last time he was there was last week to grab a shirt. He also found out that when his parents and sister moved in before he was born they found a XXL shirt hanging in the same closet and they said it did not belong to anyone in the house. I mean that might be nothing but just the fact that it was from the same closet. The last thing my friend told me awhile back that could relate to this is he was sleeping and he heard his name and woke up. No one was in his room or anything. I don't know what this thing is but its there and his mom knows it's there as well. What could it be?

Answer

Remove this entity as soon as possible. The tearing up, pressure and being momentarily paralyzed are all signs of a spirit/demon trying to communicate through your body and seeking possession of your body.

It is not something you want around. No link to any family that I can see. For your safety it is best not to do what it wants.

Follow-up Question

Okay. Thank you! And another thing, we set up

white noise on his television to see if anything would happen and my friend was talking about how he read up and you can hear the dead. We were talking and the television randomly just shut off. We tried to come up with an explanation. The remote was on the other side of the room inside his dresser. There's no timer on the TV either so there's no explanation. It happened when we were talking about it. So tonight were going to set up 2 cameras and tape for an hour at 3am (dead time). Were also going to set up a 6 hour VHS tape on and record on his TV and leave white noise running to see if anything happens. I will let you know if anything else happens. I'm glad you believe us because no one else does. We also found out a little boy died in his backyard from drowning in the pool from the previous owners...and a priest used to live in this house. I cannot remember what the last thing the house was used for his mom said something like a church. Also realizing my friend was in a incident this year and he said this is the most negativity he has had and depression he has brought to the house. We are thinking this is why its happening. Well thanks again and I hope you follow up on this email.

Answer

The television turning off will happen either by the ghost or as a projected thought from someone

in the area of the television If you have someone helping you that does not want to do this bad
enough it could happen.

You should be able to record the ghost if that
is what it wants.

Follow-up Question

Okay, and what do you mean "If you have someone helping that does not want to help it could
happen?" He just sent me a video on a text mes-
sage of his cat. His car is meowing really loud and
its on his bed just starring at his closet. It keeps
looking there and just is stiff. On top of that I
forgot to mention before my friend left for school
this morning this fan was in front of the closet door, and the closet door was shut. He came
home and the closet door was open yet again and
the fan was moved...his parents said they did not
touch the fan or go in his room.

Answer

Yes that is what I mean. The mind is a very
powerful.

Shaking Me Awake

Question

GHOSTS and other unseen visitors

How can I get rid of a male presence in my bed-room, I have seen him once appear and disappear, and he was in my face once, he pounces on my bed, jiggles my bi-pap hose up and down and now has recently started shaking me awake, usually between the hours of 11 pm anytime through 5 am some nights he does not appear, sometime a few time, others he torments me awake all through the night. I need help.

Answer

You need to be stern and mean what you say when talking with this ghost. Tell him to leave the same as you would any unwanted visitor. It may take a few times of stating what you want for it to work. Confidence and belief in yourself is key. You can also use a nightlight in your room to deter the ghost.

If you do not have enough confidence to use the above method you can burn sage to clear your space while repeating your command for the ghost to leave. Use the nightlight also for extra measure.

Small Appliances Turning On

Question

I first moved to this house may of last year and I kept seeing something in the hallway and my brother also saw this I had been through bit of rough break up before I moved and things settled down within about 2 months of being here till recently.

I have had the television turn itself on and off in front of me twice the microwave ting on few occasions I have heard phone ringing and kids toys going off on there own and today has probably been the worst I went to ring my daughter off my mobile but her phone did not ring I heard a lot of background noise so called out her name but I got a woman the other end of the phone she told me I knew who she was but I did not know the voice she eventually told me her name was Diane but I don't know a Diane she was adamant I knew her then she said to me that I did know her she was my mother well not my mother but wife was her exact words to be honest I was that freaked out I hung up and tried to ring my daughter again this time I got her but she couldn't hear anything I said cos of the static on the phone, same when I tried to call my friend back, not sure would just like some help feel like I have lost the plot.

Answer

You have a troubled spirit in your house. You do

not know this spirit. It just wants your attention and it has succeeded. Do not look into it further because that is what it wants. There is no plot, or story or meaning. It just wants your attention.

Spirits that are confused after death will linger on and life will often become even more confusing to them, they will cause problems because they know this will get them the attention they want. Your acknowledgment of them makes them feel "still alive".

The best thing to do is to direct them toward the light. I say them because as I write this to you I see more than one in your home. You need to be firm and confident in your desire for them to be gone. If you are not confident it may not work. You can use tools such as incense, candles, night lights to enforce your commands.

Astral Projection

Question

Lately I have been seeing spirits in the form of my 21 year old son and my fifty year old sister. Approximately, two weeks ago at around 2:30am while laying in my bed awake I heard a door which my son gain entry to the house opened. My bedroom door was opened and I saw my son passed to go to his room. I called out to him and received no response so I decided to go after him to his room. When I got there he was not there, I searched the entire house and he was not in the house. About four nights after around the same time I got up to use the bathroom and in doing so I passed by son's bedroom and saw him laying in his bed (he sleeps with the door ajar). I used the bath and went back to bed, when I awoke around 6am to get ready for work I saw that my son was not in his bed. During the day I phoned him and asked him what time did he leave the house only to be told that he was not home last night he slept at his studio miles away. Now here is where I became concerned because I know I did see him in his bed, I know I was not asleep but fully awake. My third encounter was two nights ago, while sleeping I felt my bedroom door being opened, it was not locked but also not ajar. When I opened my eyes I saw my sister passing to go towards the front of the house (bathroom, kitchen, living room). I decided to go after her to see if it was really her. When I did so she was nowhere there. I questioned her about it and she said she was not up then. I know it's spirits I am seeing but I want to know why I am seeing them in the form of my son and sister? Is this natural?

Answer

Sometime when we sleep we leave our body and

GHOSTS and other unseen visitors

travel to other places. Most likely this is what you are seeing, your son and your sister during times of travel while sleeping, referred to as astral projection.

You may want to ask them if they were sleeping during these times just for confirmation.

Objects Moving

Question

I am really concerned or better yet intrigued by a pattern of actions taking place at my mom's house that are just paranormal. Her stove turns on now and then without anyone near it. Items from her kitchen island are being dropped on the floor, and my son at the age of 3 did in fact see someone come down the stairs and got really scared. He is the only one to see this so called ghost. My question is because in these last 2 weeks we have had something very unusual happen and I need to know if this is even possible. My kids playing sofa appeared ALL WET with a slimy type of liquid. A LOT as if someone had poured a whole bucket on it. This had no odor, and was soaking wet. Nothing else was wet around it, and no leak anywhere since this was in the middle of the living room. Then 2 days ago the same type of liquid appeared on the big family coach. Same thing. Tremendous amount, slimy, no odor and only in the middle of the coach. Again no leak, no windows, and just on that spot. There was no one in the house when these 2 episodes occurred. We at first thought it might be our cat. But I checked with our vet and they don't think this has anything to do with the cat. She is hardly inside anyway, but we are trying to find a logical explanation. Can you please tell me if this would be something a ghost might do? Have you ever seen something like this? ON one occasion we did find a bathroom Matt all wet inside the bathroom. No one ever uses that bathroom, there had been no kids, and also no leak and no water any where around. But then again it inside a bathroom so we thought it could very well be water. But now this happens so we are strongly believing this ghost wants to be noticed.

Please let me know what you think. We do not know who to go to.

Thank you in advance for your time.

Answer

This is highly possible if you have looked for a logical explanation with no results. A ghost will do this to get attention and to be noticed. Things falling to the floor, appliances turned on or items put elsewhere, are all things a ghost can do.

Children are usually the first to see ghosts.

If you want it to stop you will need to do a clearing using some sage/incense. Walk through the house with the lit incense or sage stick, making sure to reach every corner and window with the smoke. This can be reinforced by placing nightlights where the most activity occurs. You may need to repeat the process several times to remove the ghost. This depends greatly on what you are dealing with and your confidence level.

Demons

Question

I would like to help My friend Chelsea be able to defend herself from these bad things, as well as focus her energy on the good things that can come from this gift. I have heard that bad demons can sometimes manifest themselves and take over a persons body. What do we do to strengthen her? And how do we meditate? Can you list the steps of Meditation? Also, I got her permission to do a house clearing, but I have some powers, in which

I don't think I will need a sage stick, but I don't know, I hold what is called the Aronic Priesthood, so I can get rid of the spirits. But one of my fears is that I may also get rid of the good spirit Chelsea believes is protecting her. Also if she is a Medium/Psychic, will this stuff really ever stop? I could really use your help, I am very interested in your line of profession, so as many questions as you can answer from this E-Mail would be awesome, as well as ANY information you can give me.

Answer

If you are aware they cannot take over your body. Knowledge is the first line of defense, 2nd would be your confidence.

Chelsea should strengthen herself through drawing down light energy from the source, claiming her power and accepting it. This will form a sphere of protection around her.

Meditation sit in a chair or lay down, close your eyes, breathe deeply and relax. Let go of thoughts that may come through. Then begin your visualization and energy work. Bring the subconscious and conscious minds together.

When you perform the clearing, if you focus on only removing lower, negative energy and spirits, the good will not be removed. If the spirit you thought was good is gone afterwords then it was not good in nature and may have been playing a trick on Chelsea. Many spirits will take on other forms to gain the trust of a person.

Being psychic/medium comes with many visitors, it does not end. It does however become much easier and your ability to discern gets better. She will reach a point where it will be like talking to a person and you just ask them to leave and they must leave. Practice with confidence.

Haunted Life

Question

Hi, I guess I just have a few questions to ask you, because I'm wondering if the things that have been happening to my friend Chelsea may be the happenings of a haunting. About a week ago, I started talking to her on facebook chat, and she began telling me that she had been having some very weird experiences since she was 6 years old. She witnessed her great grandfather almost die when she was only 6 years old, and she says when the hospital took him into their care that my friend Chelsea was the only one he remembered. She is now almost 18 years old, and she is still having terrible and frighting experiences. I will give a list of her experiences that she has told me.

1. She says that every night recently in the past 2 weeks, that she has had this immense pressure all over her body, so hard an full that she cannot move or speak, she says that it feels like she is being pushed into her bed, and she will just keep repeating a bible verse in her head until it goes away. I have done some research on this, and found that it may be sleep paralysis, but with all of the other stuff that has been happening to her, I have basically ruled this out.

2. She has witnessed a can being thrown across the kitchen.

3. She sees this black mass over her she says at least 3-5 times a week.

4. She has seen several apparitions. She says that she has seen a little girl sitting in the corner of her room repeating the same thing over and over "it is not over yet. It is not over yet". Chelsea says that she repeated the bible verse in her head, and then the little girl grunted and went away. The other apparition she has seen is her great grandfather. She says that she saw him walk through the kitchen wall, and she went to check it out, and no one was there. She believes that her great grandfathers

spirit is protecting her, and she feels him tugging at her sleeve, and brushing her hair. She also says that she can feel it when he goes away, and the bad feeling comes back. She says when it happens that it gets really cold, and then the black mass will come back. She says that when she lived in her old house around the time she was 8 or 9, that her gas stove would turn on, and her and her sister went into a deep sleep, her mom got home from work only to find that all of the burners on the stove had been turned on, and if her mom had not got home in time, she and her sister would probably be dead. She lives in a brand new house now, so I don't think these experiences are linked to her house, which brings the worse to mind, that these things happening to her may be a demon. I'm very afraid for her, as I'm worried that these things are getting worse. Anything you can do to help would be very much appreciated. I have tried to contact other people about this matter. But all of them have failed to respond. I hope you can help. Thank you for your time and consideration.

Answer

Your friend needs to strengthen her inner self to remove this from her life.

The immense pressure on her body is a lower entity/demon. As is the dark mass she sees. They are attracted to her because she is sensitive and she can see and hear them.

Follow-up Question

So what do we do now. This is really scaring her. Are there ways that I can help her?

Answer

You can use energy to clear her space and surroundings. This can only be done with her permission otherwise it will not work.

Get a sage stick and use it to clear her space and around her body. You can get sage sticks from local health stores. Light it and move the smoke around her and her space (home). For an extra boost light a few white candles and let them burn. You can use the 7 day candles available at your local store. After this the area will be cleansed. You may need to repeat the process a few times before it is completely cleared and all entities are gone.

You can enforce this by adding nightlights to frequently visited areas of the home.

If you are good at visualizing you can see the area cleared and will it to stay clear.

Follow-up Question

I hope I'm not bothering you. But I still have so many more questions! I want to know if these things can affect me when I'm around her, and if you are suggesting to me that my friend Chelsea is some kind of Medium, or psychic or something. If so, are there ways to develop these things?

Answer

Yes, you can be affected. But the more aware you are of them the less they will be able to influence you. Chelsea is special in that she has the ability to see, hear and feel these beings. Of course this does come with a downside. She needs to look in herself for strength, to tap into the inner power. Chelsea is more able to access her inner power due to her sensitivity.

Yes this can be developed through meditation. Meditation taps into the subconscious bringing it closer to the conscious waking mind. When these two forces (the conscious and subconscious mind) are brought together the power manifests outwardly into super human abilities. Of course everyone is different. Some may tap into it the first time they meditate while others may take a while longer to see results.

Something In My Bed

Question

When I'm off to bed, turn off the lights. I feel like there is someone lying next to me and I hear deep breathing sounds and when I turn the lights back on and I don't hear anything and this repeats the entire night till I ignore it and sleep. My sister have heard very heavy footsteps.(me and my sister have separate rooms and this only happens on the top floor)Is this some sort of paranormal activity? If yes, is there a way out? Thanks

Answer

You can perform a house clearing by using incense or a sage stick and burning it in the house. Take the lit incense and walk through the house making sure to reach all corners, doorways and windows, this may need to be repeated for several days. If that does not work you may have a stubborn ghost that does not want to leave in which case you can express your want for the ghost to leave just by telling it to leave. Always remember not to express fear in any way. State your intent firmly.

If you still have problems you may need a professional to clear your home.

Follow-up Question

Thanks a lot for your prompt reply.

This happens in my husband's home built in the late 90's. From what I know its just he and his sister who have experienced it. They suspect its done by someone (an enemy) by sending in a spirit. I get sick whenever I live there without my husband around. Presently my in laws are living in that house, they use the ground floor, so they don't face any such situation.

(the first question was posted by my husband)

Thanks

Answer

Yes, it could very well be someone alive sending in the energy. If you have an idea of who it maybe you can certainly put a stop to it by merely visualizing a shield of white light all the way around the home, inside and out, then, in a firm voice, request all energy being sent to you to be returned to the sender. You may need to do this a few times. The shield of light, when maintained will repel all further energy from getting in.

Child Seeing Ghosts

Question

My child has always been seeing ghost some are scary and others are relatives or friendly, I do not know how to help her she is extremely scared at times. Please help me, I have no one to ask, people are always making her feel bad.

Answer

Educate yourself on what your child is going through. The local library is a good start. The more you know the better you will be able to help.

Before bed surround your child with a white light through meditation.

Cold Spots

Question

Since I moved to my apt a little over 2 years ago a lot of unexplained. Things have happened such as things randomly falling and one day when I woke up there was an inflatable sled hanging in front of my kids door by a very thin thread, it was looped around the eaves of the door. No one would fess up to it. I have seen a black shadow run by my bedroom door and felt a cold spot in my kitchen on a hot day. I have heard footsteps in my back stairwell when no one was there. My house is 100 years old and I don't know if anyone died here. It is giving me the creeps and I would like to know how to tell for sure if it is a ghost or something else.

Answer

Seeing shadows and having cold spots usually means a ghost is there.

A death in the home does not necessarily mean that the person will haunt the space. There are many souls that just travel around.

You may want to research the history of the home and the land the house sits on.

Sensitive Dog

Question

For more than a week now my dog has been acting very odd in the kitchen. There are times when she wont go in or stands and the doorway staring and shaking. The first time it happened I thought maybe the light was too bright for her in there and had her eyes checked out by a specialist. I have used sage and smudged a few times but it seems to only help momentarily. What can I do and do I have anything to be concerned about?

Answer

You need to be consistent. Try a cleanse for a week. State your intent during the cleansing, once each day and see if that does it. If that does not work you may need outside help.

Monster

Question

My family moved into a house 6 months ago, just this week my oldest son 4 started seeing this thing. He calls it a monster. Today I went into the kid's room there is three lights in there. I went in to get them up and the one light bulb was unscrewed enough to not work the other on. I fixed it. then when I put them to bed all the bulbs were unscrewed. My wife sees the same thing my kids do. why does it seem to be around but I cannot see it.

Answer

It does not want you to know it is there. Do not allow this to happen. Use my three step removal.

Electrical Energy

Question

Why would an energy being that has crossed over want you to feel their energy? Many years ago, I was staying in an old apartment in NYC for the summer. One night I woke up and saw at a distance a silhouette of a man in his 20's. He was just looking at me. I kept looking back as I could not believe what I was seeing. Finally, believing that it was just my imagination, I dozed off. I woke up again and felt this presence over me. Then I felt this electrical energy go through my body and then disappear. I never saw or felt this energy again. Why did this happen?

Answer

This a personal experience that was meant just for you. The answer to this is within you and will become apparent at a later date.

You have connections of another worldly nature.

Follow-up Question

Thank you for your reply. But please specify what you mean when you said I have connections of another worldly nature?? I have had many experiences with sensing energies mostly positive and very few negative, fortunately, I have always been able to protect myself and others. But I am intrigued with what you mean by your statement. I look forward to your reply. Thanks and kind regards.

Answer

You have strong connections to places other

than the earth. Your experience was one such encounter.

Negative Energy

Question

I have been having some thoughts that I probably have a spirit or negative energy in my house. My husband seems to hear and see it more than others in the house. I myself haven't seen anything but have heard things and have had lights surge before. My children have also seen things and say our house is haunted it seems to try and scare them more. My husband has heard growling and hears distinct kicking on the bedroom door when nobody is around. I myself do not feel as it so negative but have to go with the family fear. I tell them to not even let it know that they know it is there and it wont bother them. My husband went and talked to a lady he says is a Voodoo priestess and says she feels the spirit is going off my energy? I my self say ok whatever but do seem to get sick allot. I refuse to let this make me feel as I'm not in control of the situation still. I believe in the Wiccans Way I guess you could say but do believe there is a God and Angels and Demons. I'm hoping that does make a little since to you. Its hard to tell without writing a book. My question I guess is how do I know what my husband isn't his imagination running wild ? I feel no harm in my way or path I do have a little Jack Russel dog who is about 8 now who seems to follow me every where I go and it may just be He is closer to me or is he protecting me? I have heard him growl at times with nothing there but that doesn't mean he is seeing a ghost he is a terrier he could hear a mouse ! I'm hoping this made some since but this is the best I can explain it without write you another book your advice would mean allot to me Thank you.

Answer

Sounds like you do have a spirit in your home. The reason you do not sense it so much is because you are ignoring it. Some spirits can take your energy and it may well be attached to you. I would recommend a thorough clearing of yourself and your home.

Anytime fear is involved it will be manipulated as an energy source for further haunting.

If you want to know for sure, personally I would find the place in your home that is most active with this energy, sit there and sense the energy. You could also ask what it is and wait for a response. The answer may come in the form of a noise, touch, inner knowing or other physical sensation.

Hearing Voices

Question

My question is about hearing voices. My mom told me for the last couple of weeks that she keeps hearing my sister's voice calling for her when my sister is not even there. This morning she heard my dad's voice who had already went to work but it was different this time. She said the voice sounded fearful like it was trying to warn her about something but she doesn't know what. Most of our family doesn't believe us, we have had unexplained things happen in their home. There's actually one room in my mom's house that my sister adamantly refuses to go into. We have seen shadowy figures walking through the kitchen, in that room my sister dislikes I have felt someone moving their hand up my leg and in her room a radio was turned off along with a light. No one was home except for me when the radio and light was turned off. My sister has heard voices in their home before but they have never sounded like someone's voice she knows. I don't live with them but I won't stay the night over there anymore because of the hand running up my leg. Until the voices started calling for my mom, she was not worried about whether there is a spirit or not. What is causing her to hear these voices?

Answer

Sounds like you have a group of spirits haunting the area. Hearing them is not uncommon. It is advised that you clear the space and add a layer of protection. Follow my three step method.

Demon Attack

Question

How can I protect my self from demonic attack when sleeping (so they won't invade or manipulate my dreams) I have awakened usually. Between 2 and 3 in the morning and have seen a black robed figure.

Answer

Just before sleep take a deep breath and close your eyes and see your space protected in the highest light, then on top of this see a blue light. Let the light spread out from your room to all around your space/home. Reinforce this by saying "my space is protected and secure from all unwanted lower energies and beings".

Follow-up Question

What are the dark entity's? Thank You

Answer

They are lower level demons.

Talking Board

Question

About 3 years ago I got into witch craft, had no idea what I was doing but still tried. I used the talking board almost every day, not knowing how to properly do it but I did not care. Eventually I threw it in the trash. Not to long after I started to see a lot of black shadows, which made me cry on the spot, it was like whenever I saw them I felt intense emotional pain. I started to hear whispers but not very often. I would have such bad nightmares of being attacked from people I knew to animals, I would wake up and still not be able to move. My best friend at the time said a few times he woke up and I was starring at him with no expression on my face, yet I never seemed to remember anything the next day. I became very violent and angry and stopped social activities and dropped out of school. Every time I would move it would follow me and I still haven't gotten rid of it. a woman I know with certain abilities said she tried to help me without me knowing and this thing attacked her. I don't know what this is but please help me! Thank you.

Answer

Unfortunately information on the use of the talking board is never given to the end user. It is a tool that attracts lower level entities, demons and other beings. Once used to summon and talk with entities things can go bad.

You have one or more entities attached to you. Clearing them out can be done with persistence, belief and faith. You must believe in yourself and your own ability to own your own life. You must demand that these entities leave.

The woman that tried to help you did not have your permission prior to helping you so of course she failed and was attacked. Universal law states that permission must be given by the recipient (You) before any clearing, healing or spiritual work may be performed.

Shadows

Question

Three times now I have seen a dark shadow in my house. Twice in my cellar where it came at me fast and disappeared in front of me. Then the other night I was walking into my living room where I saw it come out of the wall and go across the room and down the back of my coach. What first came to mind was I was not supposed to see it and how fast it was. It occurred to me the next day that every place I have lived since I was young, I have seen things and have had things happen, what is your opinion.

Answer

You are one of the few that have the ability to see entities. Many unseen entities are drawn to sensitive people such as yourself. Some just want to be acknowledged. If it is not causing trouble for you then most likely it just wants you to know it is there.

Ghost Cat

Question

I think I have a ghost cat, I can feel something jump on the bed, I and other people have seen a black shadow in the shape of cat moving around the house, primarily the upstairs.

Answer

It is not uncommon to have an animal ghost. They also seek companionship in the hereafter. It may be a pet from the past.

Dead Uncle

Question

I have never had any of what I might consider psychic experiences until this last year.

I found out my uncle died. I did not know the man very well, but since I was a child I was drawn to him. He seemed to be a kind, gentle man.

A month went by and as usual on a Monday morning, I go to work. I came home for lunch, ate, and went out the front door to go back to work and I stopped -- something told me I had to go to the back porch. I couldn't leave... so I unlock the door, go through the house, out the back door, and find the freezer we keep on the back porch wide open. My husband had left it open when he took ice out to fill the cooler that morning (he left on a trip).

Feeling a little strange I closed the door and took off for work. When I came home that afternoon, I went over to the mailbox to collect the mail... I look down to the ground and I saw a gold ring. Picking it up I realized it was a diamond wedding band! I found the owner of the ring and gave it back (granddaughter had lost it several weeks prior - mementos from her parents marriage). I had never seen her with this ring.

I went to bed that night and woke up because I felt there was someone standing beside me. I was not frightened, because I knew who it was - it was my uncle. I did not see him, but rather felt his presence. I did not open my eyes, either (I wear a "mask" at night, as any light greatly bothers me). I remember I smiled, and felt very happy he was there... and I went back to sleep. That was the last time I felt his presence.

There is something else that happened, but I don't want to go into too much detail. Just let me say that one of my parents was isolated from the family due to a brother (elderly abuse). My parent died without the family knowing and we were never informed. Parent was moved to an undisclosed place, died, and was secretly buried. One night, again my husband gone on a trip, I was sitting watching TV thinking 'I have to go bed.' I start to stand up and I 'hear' my parent whisper my name... I knew immediately I had to get up, go to the computer, and put in my parent's name. When I did this, my parent's obituary was the first listed. This was a month and a half after death.

I haven't had anything further happen. I do know that the 'voice' and 'feeling' my uncle was standing by me both occurred on the left side -- the left side of my brain, that is. When my parent spoke, I could feel the 'energy' in the left lobe.

What do you make of all this?

Answer

This is normal for a sensitive person. You are communicating with the after life. Spirits can communicate with you through thoughts. There may be something you need to know and you will know.

Trapped

Question

Last night when I was sleeping, I had what I thought was a dream, I felt very scared and then tried to wake myself up, I couldn't breath, my arms felt pinned down and I felt very trapped. When I was finally able to scream and catch my breath, I had a very bad feeling. My house has never felt scary to me before, I have had a few other nights like this night but put it off as a nightmare. I don't know what to think, my husband doesn't seem to believe it was anything other than a dream, do you have any advice on what it could be. I know it is a very minor incident, but one I don't want to happen again.

Answer

There are several levels of consciousness we go through before actual sleep and in those states we can encounter spirits/ghosts/other beings. In these levels you are vulnerable. Most people awake to not even have any recollection of this. Most may have strange thoughts or feelings and do not know why.

You must treat it as you would any other unwanted encounter. Protect your self and your space through intent using incense and other tools that you are comfortable using.

Noises at Night

Question

My son is 8 years old. For the past 3 years, he has said he hears noises at night. He can't see the noise, but only hear it. He hears it every night about 3 am. It only happens when everyone in the house is sleeping. He has been very descriptive. He has said that it sounds like someone is walking down the hall wearing wind pants. The noise always walks around his bed. It touches his feet. He said a couple times that it sounds like the person was standing next to his bed with a plastic bag and a book, and was going to put the book in the bag. He is so scared at night that he has to have his radio really loud to avoid hearing the noise. He puts two pillows at the foot of his bed with thick fleece blankets on top of the pillows - just so he doesn't feel the noise touch his feet. He has a night lamp and a night light on every night. His curtains have to be open. His closet doors have to be shut. His bedroom door has to be open. We have done numerous things to help reassure him that he is safe. We have walked through the house to show him there is nothing in our house that will hurt him. He says he can't see the noise so walking through the house doesn't help. We have read books about God. He has told the noise to leave him alone. He's said a prayer to God. He has an Indian dream catcher next to his door as well as a cross, but he still hears the noise. We had our house blessed by our Father a week ago. After that, my son said he doesn't understand why he still hears the noise because the noise should be gone now that our house is blessed. He said the noise is worse now and he thinks the devil is in our house. A little background ... we built our house 3 years ago. We had a puppy who died for unknown reasons 2 years ago. We now have a new puppy. We live on the outskirts of town so I wonder if something maybe happened on this land. I don't know if the noise could be our dead puppy's spirits because it won't leave and it always walks around my son's bed. My son and puppy were pretty close so it was devastating when our puppy passed away. We do not know what to do. Our son is awake every night from approximately 3 am. to 5 am. due to the noise. I wake every morning to my son sleeping on my bedroom floor. I want him to feel safe and secure in his bedroom but I don't foresee that happening any time soon. Do you have any suggestions of what we can do to help him? Your help will be GREATLY appreciated!!!!!

Answer

The Father that blessed the house may not have had the experience or belief to get the job done. Of course the spirit is mad now because you are attempting to remove it. You can assure your son that it is not the devil. It may want you to believe that but it is not. It is not the puppy that has passed away.

You need to do the following for three days at the same time each night.

Take a white candle and light it and place it in the center of the room. Take either incense or a sage wand the light it now walk around the room making sure the smoke surrounds all areas your son refers to as being hot spots. While using the incense repeat "This space is free and clear of all lower entities and lower influences, only the highest light and love may enter this space". Do this for three nights at the same time. You may also add crystals to each corner of the space. Another trick is to place salt around the perimeter.

If you are not confident enough to carry this out it may not work. Approach this the same way you would if a person you did not want in your home was in your home. Be firm and confident.

If you would like me to clear the space remotely just write me back.

Follow-up Question

Thank you for your prompt response. We plan to go shopping tomorrow and buy everything you suggested. We will start this tomorrow night and do it for the next 3 nights. I really hope it works. After watching some shows on TV about ghosts (we watched Ghost Adventures last night and they were dealing with demonic entities), I have to admit that I am a bit nervous about this. I hate that a spirit wants to cause fear in my son. He has been through a lot already. We discovered this past January that he had a rare brain tumor. We are lucky we caught it when we did because the doctors said it wouldn't have been much time before he would have gone into a coma. He had the brain tumor removed and subsequently had 4 shunt surgeries from February through the middle of April. He is doing well health wise now but it's frustrating that there's a spirit that wants to cause him fear. He's already afraid of lots of things. Where did this spirit come from? Why would it want to cause him fear? Will it do anything to my other two children? I have a 6 year old daughter and 3 month old daughter. Is this spirit something my dog would sense is in here?

We will come together as a family and be strong and face this spirit. I refuse to let anything cause him fear any longer. I will be strong, firm, and confident because I have had enough.

Would it be beneficial to have you clear the space remotely and have us do it too?

Again, sincere thanks and appreciation for all your help!!!

Answer

Do not be nervous. You have the power over this entity. It is fear that they feed on and cause.

If it still persists after you clear the space for three days let me know and I will get rid of it.

Watch your other children for:

1. Nightmares

2. Make believe friends.

3. Talking to someone at night that is not there.

4. Unusual change in mood or behavior.

These are signs that should be addressed with a clearing.

Animals are quite aware and will sense subtle energy influxes so the answer is yes your dog may sense a presence that you do not. Watch for barking, growling, whining, or nervousness at something you cannot see.

Spirits Talking

Question

ok I have never done anything like this before but im going to give it a shot, its not really a question but in a way it is. My names is danielle I am 20 yrs old I have a 15 yr old sister who is native american and she is not in total health. Last year she told me that she had been seeing people in her room and she said they were talking to her. Anyone in there right mind would be scared right ? Just a few days ago she told me about this dream she had, she said " I was in the basement " which is weird cause she never ever goes down there. She told me a man wearing black pants and black gloves and a white shirt grabbed her arm and she tried so hard to see his face but it was like he didnt have one. She also told me he talked to her and told her that there are 3 spirits in our home, 2 little girls which is weird cause my dad says there are 2 little girls here too. He can hear them playing when no one is home. She also said that the man told her there is one other spirit it is in our home. It is in her room and its not there to hurt her its there to protect her. After the man in her dream told her that she woke up. I was wondering if you could tell me if any of this has any significant meaning. If there is something here we would like to contact whom ever they may be. Could you tell us how to do that?

Answer

The man without the face is not to be trusted. There is another spirit in the house. I would suggest a complete house clearing. Contacting this spirit is not a good idea. Many times when someone is in a weakened state there will be dark spirits about that will try to gain trust. Higher beings will never appear without a face.

Demonic Attack

Question

I've been attacked by "shadow men" both physically and mentally. They've tried to posses me twice, but faild. Is this because I have the holy spirit?

Answer

Whenever you are drawing light to yourself (holy spirit, god) you will get noticed and challenged until you can master protection. The best thing to do is to intend a light of protection around yourself and your surroundings. Even a deep cleansing of your home will help.

Follow-up Question

Hey, I have been using olive oil and have been speaking barriers around the home and the nightmares stop, or if they come something inside me takes control of the dream and makes me yell at them about Jesus and his blood. These shadows cringe, hide, and angrily scoff but they give up. The only avenue this spirit of Jezebel is using now is my god-given sex drive. It seems overpowering and distorts my view of women. Especially porn. Any things you know of that could help? I know Paul had this problem too.

Answer

Rid your home of these items. Also professional help may be needed if you are unable to refrain from these activities. Will power and determination are needed.

Unexplained Happenings

Question

I constantly see things running past my windows, I see them quite frequently. Ive seen shadows of footprints with no person there. My older sister woke up one night with a intense pain in her arm, she looked down and there was a hand print bruised in her arm. It was on her left arm with a left hand print. Ive woke up with scratches on my legs and arms. Ive woke up in the middle of the night out of breath and my dream was that somebody was holding my down but im not so sure it was a dream. I just want answers please and thank you.

Answer

You have demons around. Try using a clearing method using smudge sticks, candles and night lights. Use the night lights after you clear your space. These have shown to help when you sleep.

Paranormal Insight

Question

I want to know if it's wise and okay to try to talk to spirits with my friend. We do respect them very much, we do not wish to harm them or be harmed. We did not and will not use any substances to contact them like ouija board. We just want to talk to them and get some history of the location. We pray the lords prayer and secure ourselves from evil before doing so. What should we do?

Answer

This is not something to do carelessly. Protection is important. If you have any doubts do not proceed. I would not use a Ouija Board.

I need help with ghosts!

Question

I need help and I need it fast please. Ive been having problems with ghost since I was 11 I am now 20 im scared its hard for me to sleep at night cause thats when it seems liek I get messed with im constantly feeling like im being watched no matter where I sleep and it feels evil not a good spirit at all ive gotten my hair pulled held down chocked etc... it doesnt happen every night but enough to where im fed up I need to know whats going on who it is and what they want from me?

Answer

It is not just one but quite a few. Now is a good time to practice protection methods. Do not be fearful because this will only make the situation worse. Gather your inner strength and self confidence, it is required. Know that you CAN make them leave. When you have a physical person in your home that you do not want there, do you let them stay or do you tell them to leave? You must treat the unseen in the same manner, tell them to leave and do not take no for an answer. Be confident, firm and unafraid.

Paranormal

Question

Something grabbed my arm and shocked me & called my name & said wake up. It was on a Sunday morning, about an hour later I received a phone call that my grandmother had past away.. After that I was bothered with something every night in my bedroom. Lights would turn on, doors would open.. It got so bad I moved to another bedroom. My husband will not sleep in there!! People think I am crazy!! I've always have had bad dreams & nightmares. What ever it was it came in my kitchen and started banging on the counter & turned lights on & off. Some say it's my mirrors. I don't know!! Prayed over my home & it's stopped for now. I still see a big ball of light every now & then..

Answer

Often when someone passes away there are lower level entities hanging around. They feed off pain, grieving and fear. They tend to show themselves during times of sadness. It is not your mirrors. You are doing right through your prayers. If the problem persists be more stern and tell them to leave as you would anyone you do not want in your house. Take back your home and your life and make them aware that they are not welcome. Do not express fear as this will only make the situation worse.

Again, you need to be stern, demanding and 100% confident when you deal with this.

CHAPTER 4

Cases

Some Client

case files

A Few Cases

Here are just a few of the cases that I have been involved with. They are not in any particular order and the names have been omitted and/or changed to protect the privacy of my clients.

The Possession of Amanda

Amanda was a distraught, depressed 16 year old living in the Midwest. Her mother contacted me by email and explained how Amanda was withdrawn, depressed and even suicidal. Her mother also explained how Amanda looked as if the life had been drained from her, she was lifeless and very pale looking.

I took the case and told the mother that I would need to assess Amanda before continuing. That nigh I assessed Amanda and diagnosed her as having an attachment (possession). An attachment is where another being holds on to a living person by means of possessing them on a soul level.

I contacted the mother and explained Amanda's condition and what I could do for her. The mother insisted that I begin the treatments.

I completed the treatments on Amanda within a week. Her mother contacted me the next week to tell me how Amanda was doing. Her mother was over joyed at how much Amanda had improved. Amanda was now social again, she wanted to go to school, she was drawing again and Amanda had the color back in her cheeks. Her mother commented on how nice her hair now looks against her rosy skin. Her mother noted that Amanda's whole outlook had changed and she thanked me for bringing back the daughter she knew just 5 years ago. Amanda also started to sketch Archangel Michael and felt a bond with him.

House Clearing

My client had a ghost in her house that liked to move items around and make noise while the family was sleeping. I agreed to take a look to assess the situation. I did see more than one ghost and told my client. She gave the go ahead so I prepared to clear the house as I normally do. In the middle of performing the clearing a demon ran at me and came nose to nose with me. It told me it was not leaving under any circumstances. Well, I beg to differ, so I proceeded with the clearing.

This is not the first time I have had an encounter like this nor will it be my last, I suspect. Due to the energy of the demons that occupied the home it took a few days to complete the clearing.

The clearing was a success and the family was

once again living in peace.

Recently Departed

An elderly woman contacted me by phone and wanted me to take a look inside her home that very minute. In no time at all I was looking into her home, I saw her on the phone and I saw another being standing in the back of the room. I told the client that an elderly gentleman was standing in the back of the room just behind her.

She suddenly was relieved and happy. She said thank you for confirming that, I thought I was going crazy. He has been here since he passed about a month ago.

Elderly Care Facility

I have always had the ability to see death within a week of happening. The soon to depart seem to have a different energy around them.

A friend of mine worked at an elderly care facility and was concerned about one of the patience there. So he took me to the facility. As we were driving out to the front an elderly woman stepped out of the door of the facility wearing a white gown. She stood there and just stared in my direction.

123

I immediately knew that she was going to pass over that night and I told my friend. When my friend went to work the next day he was told that the woman had indeed passed on in the night.

CHAPTER 5

Help

Removal Methods

Protection

Grids

Help

Why Me?

You may be asking yourself, why me? There are many reasons for attracting the unseen into your life. The most common are:

1. Alcohol and drug abuse.
2. Depression and grief.
3. Anger and violence.
4. Illness and weakness.
5. You are psychic/medium.
6. You moved into a place already haunted.

This is not a complete list, these are your guidelines. All of these items will cause you to be the target of ghosts, demons and other unseen visitors. Why? Because most of the unseen visitors have one thing in common, they love suffering, they are drawn to it like a moth to the light. If you are psychic/medium then the reason for their presence is that they know you can see and hear them and they love the attention.

Possession/Attachments

Possessions can happen when you are in a weakened state, either emotionally or physically. Self doubt, loathing, anger, grief, low self esteem can all contribute to the problem and make you very vulnerable. Once you begin feeling this way you make it easier to be influenced by the unseen. Soon your thoughts are hijacked and manipulated. You will not notice it because you were already feeling this way from the start. Friends and family will notice the drastic changes in you first. It is a good idea to listen to your friends and family and take those are warning signs. The most common characteristics of a possession/attachments are:

1. Withdraw from friends and family, you were social and now you are not.

2. Severe depression with thoughts of suicide and self mutilation. Acting on these is a sign of progressed possession.

3. Sudden change in personality. In just a few days or hours.

4. Increased substance abuse.

5. Skin color change. Looking like the life has been drained from you.

6. Sudden lack of interest in your usual interests.

7. Anger outbursts. More than usual.

Any sudden changes in how you usually are should be looked into. It is a good idea to see a counselor/psychiatrist to rule out any mental disorder before you decide you have a possession/attachment. If you can find a medium that specializes in this area you could also get an assessment.

The unseen likes something they can work with so low feelings and substance abuse can make you very vulnerable.

Tools For Focus

In the beginning it is useful to have a focal point when performing your clearings. That is all tools are used for, as a focal point. When performing a clearing it is your intent and energy that gets the job done, not the tools used. As you become more confident in your ability to direct your intent you will need these tools less and less.

1. Incense, sage wand.

2. Candles, preferably white.

3. Crystals, naturally occurring stone.

4. Nightlights, especially useful if you have young children. This item can be used always.

The use of these items will help you to become more proficient in your clearings.

Three Step Removal

You can adjust this to suit you as long as you adhere to the three steps. Some of you will need to add tools as an aid to focus on and direct your energy. Tools will also help build your confidence as you move forward.

Ready? Did you bring your confidence? The degree in which your clearing is effective depends completely on your confidence level. If you are really scared, do not proceed and find someone who is not scared to complete the clearing. You could also educate yourself on the subject of ghosts further, knowledge is power and it is a lack of knowledge on something that causes a fear on that something.

Confidence is key! Do not second guess yourself or question whether or not it worked. It did work. Thoughts to the contrary will destroy what you completed.

The three steps are:

Step one: Prepare and gather your tools. Light some candles. Light your sage or incense and use it to clear the energy of the person or space by placing it in or around the area to be cleansed. If it is a whole house you can go through each room with the incense/sage lit, making sure to go around windows, doors and corners. While doing this repeat your intent, you could say aloud, "this _____ is clear and free from all unwanted lower energies and beings". Replace the blank with person or home or whatever suits your situation. You can create your own intent to say aloud making it that much more powerful. Then place your incense/sage in a central location to the person or space you are clearing.

Step two: Close your eyes and see the space and/or person clear of all possession/attachment. Imagine it in your mind as being complete.

Step three: Give thanks for any help you have received.

Important: Repeat for three consecutive nights.

Advanced Method

Go into meditation and/or prayer and demand the unseen leave immediately. Use your energy to force the exit. Always a good idea to repeat this process for three consecutive nights.

Very Advanced Method

Feeling confident and unafraid? Just tell whatever it is to leave in a stern voice. Same as you would tell an intruder to leave that you did not want around. This always works when it is backed by your full confidence. I would not do this if you are the least bit unsure or scared.

How Archangels Can Help

On more than one case I have had the help of Archangel Michael. You can too. You just have to ask. Yes, that is all you have to do, just ask. You can pray/meditate to ask or you can just ask aloud.

The Archangels are not allowed to help in any situation unless they are invited by you.

Why Archangel Michael? He is the one Archangel that can really help in this situation. His strength in this area is unmatched.

Create a Physical Grid of Protection

Get 4 crystals (this is assuming you live in a square house), any size will work, meditate/pray with them in your hands and put the energy of protection in the crystals, be clear on your intent.

Take the crystals and place them, one in each corner of a room or the whole house (the four corners of the house).

You may need to cleanse and re-insert your intent in the crystals about every 4-12 weeks depending on your situation.

Create an Invisible Grid of Protection

This is a very effective way to protect your home and family when you cannot be right there or before you go to bed at night.

Meditate/pray and see a brilliant white light in your mind around the person or your home or even just one room. Stay focused and do not let your thoughts wander. See the light expanding about 2-10 feet from around the person or your home. Hold it in your mind for a few minutes. You can strengthen the protection by saying "only the highest light and love is within this light of protection". You can play with it and make your own verse to use which will strengthen your grid of protection. Then let it go.

This is a handy tool that you can use where ever you are and at any time of the day.

The Most Important Tool

The belief in yourself and your confidence to complete the task will serve you in being successful in removing unseen visitors. Fear has no place here. Fear will only hinder your progress. So march forth with your confidence and put an end to the visits.

CHAPTER 6

Definitions

terms

used

frequently

Definitions

Attachment

An emotional connection. Attachment involves being dependent on someone for something: emotional, mental or physical.

Apparition

Generally, an apparition is an instance of something's appearing, i.e. being seen.

Channeling, Channel

In the latter half of the 20th century, Western mediumship developed in two different ways. One type involves psychics or sensitives who claim to speak to spirits and then relay what they hear to their clients. Clairvoyant Danielle Egnew is known for her alleged communication with angelic entities.

The other incarnation of non-physical mediumship is a form of channeling in which the channeler goes into a trance, or "leaves their body". He or she becomes "possessed" by a specific spirit (spirit possession), who then talks through them. In the trance, the medium enters a cataleptic state marked by extreme rigidity. As the control spirit takes over, the medium's voice may change completely.

Clearing – See Exorcism

Crystals

A homogenous solid formed by a repeating, three-dimensional pattern of atoms, ions, or molecules and having smooth external surfaces with characteristic angles between them. Crystals can occur in many sizes and shapes.

Energy Transfer

Is the transfer of energy from one body to another.

Exorcism

(from Late Latin exorcismus, from Greek, exorkismos - binding by oath) is the religious practice of evicting demons or other spiritual entities from a person or place which they are believed to have possessed. Depending on the spiritual beliefs of the exorcist, this may be done by causing the entity to swear an oath, performing an elaborate ritual, or simply by commanding it to depart in the name of a higher power. The practice is quite ancient and part of the belief system of many cultures and religions.

Ghost

In traditional belief, a ghost is the soul or spirit of a deceased person or animal that can appear, in visible form or other manifestation, to the living.

Greys

Are alleged extraterrestrial beings whose existence is promoted in ufological, paranormal, and New Age communities, named for their skin color.

Grid

The sense of grid is as a network, and should not be taken to imply a particular physical layout, or breadth. Grid may be used to refer to an entire continent's electrical network, a regional transmission network or may be used to describe a subnetwork such as a local utility's transmission grid or distribution grid.

Incense

Incense (Latin: incendere, "to burn") is composed of aromatic biotic materials, which release fragrant smoke when burned. The term "incense" refers to the substance itself, rather than to the odor that it produces. It is used in religious ceremonies, ritual purification, aromatherapy, meditation, for creating a mood, and for masking bad odours. The use of incense may have originated in Ancient Egypt, where the gum resins and oleo gum resins of aromatic trees were imported from the Arabian and Somali coasts to be used in religious ceremonies.

Meditation

Refers to any of a family of practices in which the practitioner trains his or her mind or self-induces a mode of consciousness in order to realize some benefit

Medium, Mediumship

Mediumship is the claimed ability of a person (the medium) to experience contact with spirits of the dead, angels, demons or other immaterial entities.

Night Terrors

also known as a sleep terror or pavor nocturnus, is a parasomnia disorder that predominantly affects children, causing feelings of terror or dread. Night terrors should not be confused with nightmares, which are bad dreams that cause the feeling of horror or fear. Children from age two to six are most prone to night terrors, and they affect about fifteen percent of all children, although people of any age may experience these Night Terrors.

Episodes may happen for a couple of weeks then suddenly disappear. The symptoms also tend to be different, like the child being unable to recall the experience, and while nearly arisen, hallucinating. Children who have night terrors are usually described as 'bolting upright' with their eyes wide open, with a look of fear and panic, and will often scream. They will usually sweat, breathe fast and have a rapid heart rate (autonomic signs). Although it seems like children are awake during a night terror, they will appear confused, will not be consolable and will not recognize others.

Possession

Is a paranormal and/or supernatural event in which it is said that spirits, gods, demons, animas, extraterrestrials, or other disincarnate or extra-terrestrial entities take control of a human body, resulting in noticeable changes in health and behaviour. The term can also describe a similar action of taking residence in an inanimate object, possibly giving it animation.

Psychic

Is a person who professes an ability to perceive information hidden from the normal senses through extrasensory perception (ESP), or is said by others to have such abilities.

Index

www.ingramcontent.com/pod-product-compliance
Lightning Source LLC
Chambersburg PA
CBHW071756090426
42737CB00012B/1838